W9-CKI-159

Animal show and Tell

Animals in Polar Regions

Élisabeth de Lambilly-Bresson

 **Gareth Stevens**
Publishing

The Polar Bear

I am a polar bear.
My white fur makes me
look like a snowbank,
and it keeps me very warm
in icy wind and water.
I am so big and strong,
I rule the North Pole!

The Whale

I am a whale.
I love to leap
out of the water
and splash
back into the waves.
When I breathe,
I spray water like a fountain.

The Seal

I am a seal.
My webbed flippers help me
swim very well,
but on land,
I can only crawl.
My favorite pasttime
is sunbathing
on snow and ice.

The Penguin

I am a penguin.
I am a bird,
but I swim instead of fly.
On the ice, I stand
and waddle on two feet.
People say I look like
I am wearing a tuxedo.

The Sled Dog

I am a sled dog.
I help people
who live near the North Pole.
I have an important job.
I pull sleds long distances
over the snow and ice.

The Walrus

I am a walrus.
I spend most of my time
in the icy Arctic Ocean.
I even sleep in the sea!
I pull my big body
out of the water
by hooking my tusks
into a floating field of ice.

The Reindeer

I am a reindeer.
The branches on my head
are called antlers.
I will pull a sled for you
over polar ice and snow.
Stories say
I pull a sleigh for Santa.
Ho! Ho! Ho!

Please visit our Web site at: www.garethstevens.com
For a free color catalog describing Gareth Stevens Publishing's
list of high-quality books, call 1-800-542-2595 (USA) or
1-800-387-3178 (Canada).

Library of Congress Cataloging-in-Publication Data

Lambilly-Bresson, Elisabeth de.
   [Sur la banquise. English]
   Animals in polar regions / Elisabeth de Lambilly-Bresson. — North American ed.
      p. cm. — (Animal show and tell)
   ISBN: 978-0-8368-8203-2 (lib. bdg.)
    1. Animals—Polar regions—Juvenile literature. I. Title.
  QL104.L3613   2007
  591.70911—dc22
                                        2007002551

This North American edition first published in 2008 by
Gareth Stevens Publishing
A Weekly Reader® Company
1 Reader's Digest Road
Pleasantville, NY 10570-7000 USA

Translation: Gini Holland
Gareth Stevens editor: Gini Holland
Gareth Stevens art direction and design: Tammy West

This edition copyright © 2008 by Gareth Stevens, Inc. Original edition copyright
© 2002 by Mango Jeunesse Press. First published as *Les animinis: Sur la banquise*
by Mango Jeunesse Press.

Printed in the United States of America

1 2 3 4 5 6 7 8 9 11 10 09 08 07